When
Theo & Ana
CARE

When Theo & Ana CARE

Written by: Joy L.S. Hoffman & Danielle S. Kleist

Illustrated by: Matthew E. Howard

Tandem Light Press
950 Herrington Rd.
Suite C128
Lawrenceville, GA 30044

Tandem Light Press paperback edition

ISBN: 979-8-9882517-1-2
Library of Congress Control Number:

PRINTED IN THE UNITED STATES OF AMERICA

The Toddler Book Series is dedicated to Hanna, CJ, Emma, & James.

Acknowledgments

Thank you to Tandem Light Press for believing in us and encouraging us to write stories about everyday children in everyday families. Thank you to our partners, John & Chris, for enthusiastically saying, "go for it!!" and not crushing our dreams. Special thanks to Hanna, CJ, Emma, & James, who inspire us every day to be better humans and parents.

-Danielle & Joy

THEO AND ANA
live in a town,

Where

COWS and PIGS
are all around.

GOATS and CHICKENS, HORSES too!

Sometimes they even step in poo.

Ana and Theo
love to play
with all the animals,
NIGHT and DAY.
But when their playing becomes too rough,
the animals show they've had
ENOUGH.

Theo
squeezed the chicken
TOO TIGHT,

And made the chicken want to fight.

He didn't know how to be a

FRIEND

And now the chicken has to mend.

Ana fell on a pig with a thud,

While jumping in the very

THICK

MUD.

If Ana wants to do no harm,

she has to play carefully on the farm.

Theo and Ana need to slow down

when

GOATS and SHEEP

are standing around.

Tugging on the

LLAMA'S EAR,

can make it run away in fear.

Ana and Theo are

LEARNING

TO CARE,

To feed the horses and brush their hair.

Their parents and grownups
are showing them how.

They even learned to

MILK A COW!

EXCITEMENT

causes them to forget,

That their energy
makes the animals upset.

Being calm and kind is a must,

To earn an animal's

LOVE AND TRUST.

When both get better at playing on the farm,

And learn to care

without doing

HARM,

Their parents promised pets in the home.

Maybe a

BUNNY OR KITTY

to comb.

The other animals
WILL STAY OUTSIDE.

Because dirt and smells
are hard to

HIDE.

But Theo and Ana can learn to care,

For animals here
and animals there.

Loving animals doesn't take much;

A QUIET VOICE,
a gentle touch.

Ana and Theo

will not forget,

How to love the

FARM OR A PET.

About the Authors

Joy Hoffman is a Korean American transracial adoptee and mother of two biracial children, one of whom is autistic. Joy worked in higher education for twenty-four years before transitioning to independent consulting.

Danielle Kleist is a Korean American transracial adoptee and mother of two biracial children. Danielle worked in higher education for over ten years before transitioning to consulting with Proof Leadership and being a stay-at-home mom.

Danielle & Joy met in 2009 and found a deep connection through their adoptee experiences. They have had a sisterhood ever since and often joke about being twins separated at birth (despite a twenty-year age difference). This book series is a labor of sisterly love.

Follow us on Facebook!
Seoul Sisters Books